FIRESIDE SERIES

Ramtha

Volume 3, No. 2

PROPHETS
OF OUR OWN
DESTINY

PROPHETS
OF OUR OWN
DESTINY

ISBN # 1-57873-114-3

JZK Publishing,
A Division of JZK, Inc.

P.O. Box 1210
Yelm, Washington 98597
360.458.5201
800.347.0439
www.ramtha.com
www.jzkpublishing.com

These series of teachings are designed for all the students of the Great Work who love the teachings of the Ram.

It is suggested that you create an ideal learning environment for study and contemplation.

Light your fireplace and get cozy. Have your wine and fine tobacco. Prepare yourself. Open your mind to learn and be genius.

FOREWORD TO THE NEW EDITION

The Fireside Series Collection Library is an ongoing library of the hottest topics of interest taught by Ramtha. These series of teachings are designed for all the students of the Great Work who love the teachings of the Ram. This library collection is also intended as a continuing learning tool for the students of Ramtha's School of Enlightenment and for everyone interested and familiar with Ramtha's teachings. In the last twenty-five years, Ramtha has continuously and methodically deepened and expanded his exposition of the nature of reality and its practical application through various disciplines. It is assumed by the publisher that the reader has attended a Beginning Retreat or workshop through Ramtha's School of Enlightenment or is at least familiar with Ramtha's instruction to his beginning class of students. This required information for beginning students is found in *Ramtha, A Beginner's Guide to Creating Reality*, revised and expanded ed. (Yelm: JZK Publishing, a division of JZK, Inc., 2000), and in *Ramtha: Creating Personal Reality*, Video ed. (Yelm: JZK Publishing, a division of JZK, Inc., 1998.)

We have included in the Fireside Series a glossary of some of the basic concepts used by Ramtha so the reader can become familiarized with these teachings. We have also included a brief introduction of Ramtha by JZ Knight that describes how all this began. Enjoy your learning and contemplation.

CONTENTS

FIGURES

Introduction to Ramtha
By JZ Knight

"In other words, his whole point of focus is to come here and to teach you to be extraordinary."

You don't have to stand for me. My name is JZ Knight and I am the rightful owner of this body, and welcome to Ramtha's school, and sit down. Thank you.

So we will start out by saying that Ramtha and I are two different people, beings. We have a common reality point and that is usually my body. I am a lot different than he is. Though we sort of look the same, we really don't look the same.

What do I say? Let's see. All of my life, ever since I was a little person, I have heard voices in my head and I have seen wonderful things that to me in my life were normal. And I was fortunate enough to have a family or a mother who was a very psychic human being, who sort of never condemned what it was that I was seeing. And I had wonderful experiences all my life, but the most important experience was that I had this deep and profound love for God, and there was a part of me that understood what that was. Later in my life I went to church and I tried to understand God from the viewpoint of religious doctrine and had a lot of difficulty with that because it was sort of in conflict with what I felt and what I knew.

Ramtha has been a part of my life ever since I was born, but I didn't know who he was and I didn't know what he was, only that there was a wonderful force that walked with me, and when I was in trouble — and had a lot of pain in my life growing up — that I always had extraordinary experiences with this being who would talk to me. And I could hear him as clearly as I can hear you if we were to have a conversation. And he helped me to understand a lot of things in my life that were sort of beyond the normal scope of what someone would give someone as advice.

It wasn't until 1977 that he appeared to me in my kitchen on a Sunday afternoon as I was making pyramids with my husband at that time, because we were into dehydrating food and we were into hiking and backpacking and all that stuff. And so I put one of these ridiculous things on my head, and at the other end of my kitchen this wonderful apparition appeared that was seven feet tall and glittery and beautiful and stark. You just don't expect at 2:30 in the afternoon that this is going to appear in your kitchen. No one is ever prepared for that. And so Ramtha at that time really made his appearance known to me.

The first thing I said to him — and I don't know where this comes from — was that "You are so beautiful. Who are you?"

And he has a smile like the sun. He is extraordinarily handsome. And he said, "My name is Ramtha the Enlightened One, and I have come to help you over the ditch." Being the simple person that I am, my immediate reaction was to look at the floor because I thought maybe something had happened to the floor, or the bomb was being dropped; I didn't know.

And it was that day forward that he became a constant in my life. And during the year of 1977 a lot of interesting things happened, to say the least. My two younger children at that time got to meet Ramtha and got to experience some incredible phenomena, as well as my husband.

Later that year, after teaching me and having some difficulty telling me what he was and me understanding, one day he said to me, "I am going to send you a runner that will bring you a set of books, and you read them because then you will know what I am." And those books were called the *Life and Teachings of the Masters of the Far East*. And so I read them and I began to understand that Ramtha was one of those beings, in a way. And that sort of took me out of the are-you-the-devil-or-are-you-God sort of category that was plaguing me at the time.

And after I got to understand him, he spent long, long moments walking into my living room, all seven feet of this beautiful being making himself comfortable on my couch, sitting down and talking to me and teaching me. And what

I didn't realize at that particular time was he already knew all the things I was going to ask and he already knew how to answer them. But I didn't know that he knew that.

So he patiently since 1977 has dealt with me in a manner by allowing me to question not his authenticity but things about myself as God, teaching me, catching me when I would get caught up in dogma or get caught up in limitation, catching me just in time and teaching me and walking me through that. And I always said, "You know, you are so patient. You know, I think it is wonderful that you are so patient." And he would just smile and say that he is 35,000 years old, what else can you do in that period of time? So it wasn't really until about ten years ago that I realized that he already knew what I was going to ask and that is why he was so patient. But as the grand teacher that he is, he allowed me the opportunity to address these issues in myself and then gave me the grace to speak to me in a way that was not presumptuous but in a way, as a true teacher would, that would allow me to come to realizations on my own.

Channeling Ramtha since late 1979 has been an experience, because how do you dress your body for — Ram is seven feet tall and he wears two robes that I have always seen him in. Even though they are the same robe, they are really beautiful so you never get tired of seeing them. The inner robe is snow white and goes all the way down to where I presume his feet are, and then he has an overrobe that is beautiful purple. But you should understand that I have really looked at the material on these robes and it is not really material. It is sort of like light. And though the light has a transparency to them, there is an understanding that what he is wearing has a reality to it.

Ramtha's face is cinnamon-colored skin, and that is the best way I can describe it. It is not really brown and it is not really white and it is not really red; it is sort of a blending of that. And he has very deep black eyes that can look into you and you know you are being looked into. He has eyebrows that look like wings of a bird that come high on his brow. He has a very square jaw and a beautiful mouth, and when he smiles you know that you are in heaven. He has long, long hands, long fingers that he uses very eloquently to demonstrate his thought.

Well, imagine then how after he taught me to get out of my body by actually pulling me out and throwing me in the tunnel, and hitting the wall of light, bouncing back, and realizing my kids were home from school and I just got through doing breakfast dishes, that getting used to missing time on this plane was really difficult, and I didn't understand what I was doing and where I was going. So we had a lot of practice sessions.

You can imagine if he walked up to you and yanked you right out of your body and threw you up to the ceiling and said now what does that view look like, and then throwing you in a tunnel — and perhaps the best way to describe it is it is a black hole into the next level — and being flung through this tunnel and hitting this white wall and having amnesia. And you have to understand, I mean, he did this to me at ten o'clock in the morning and when I came back off of the white wall it was 4:30. So I had a real problem in trying to adjust with the time that was missing here. So we had a long time in teaching me how to do that, and it was fun and frolic and absolutely terrifying at moments.

But what he was getting me ready to do was to teach me something that I had already agreed to prior to this incarnation, and that my destiny in this life was not just to marry and to have children and to do well in life but to overcome the adversity to let what was previously planned happen, and that happening including an extraordinary consciousness, which he is.

Trying to dress my body for Ramtha was a joke. I didn't know what to do. The first time we had a channeling session I wore heels and a skirt and, you know, I thought I was going to church. So you can imagine, if you have got a little time to study him, how he would appear dressed up in a business suit with heels on, which he has never walked in in his life.

But I guess the point that I want to tell you is that it is really difficult to talk to people — and perhaps someday I will get to do that with you, and understanding that you have gotten to meet Ramtha and know his mind and know his love and know his power — and how to understand that I am not him, and though I am working diligently on it, that we are two separate beings and that when you talk to me in this body, you are talking to me and not him. And sometimes over the past decade or so, that has been a great challenge to me in the public media because people don't understand how it is possible that a human being can be endowed with a divine mind and yet be separate from it.

So I wanted you to know that although you see Ramtha out here in my body, it is my body, but he doesn't look anything like this. But his appearance in the body doesn't lessen the magnitude of who and what he is. And you should also know that when we do talk, when you start asking me about things that he said, I may not have a clue about what you are talking about because when I leave my body in a few minutes, I am gone to a whole other time and another place that I don't have cognizant memory of. And however long he spends with you today, to me that will maybe be about five minutes or three minutes, and when I come back to my body, this whole time of this whole day has passed and I wasn't a part of it. And I didn't hear what he said to you and I don't know what he did out here. When I come back, my body is exhausted and it is hard to get up the stairs sometimes to change to make myself more presentable for what the day is bringing me, or what is left of the day.

You should also understand as beginning students, one thing that became really obvious over the years, that he has showed me a lot of wonderful things that I suppose people who have never got to see them couldn't even dream of in their wildest dreams. And I have seen the twenty-third universe and I have met extraordinary beings and I have seen life come and go. I have watched generations be born and live and pass in a matter of moments. I have been exposed to historical events to help me to understand better what it was I needed to know. I have been allowed to walk beside my body in other lifetimes and watch how I was and who I was, and I have been allowed to see the other side of death. So these are cherished and privileged opportunities that somewhere in my life I earned the right to have them in my life. To speak of them to other people is, in a way, disenchanting because it is difficult to convey to people who have never been to those places what it is. And I try my best as a storyteller to tell them and still fall short of it.

But I know that the reason that he works with his students the way that he does is because also Ramtha never wants to overshadow any of you. In other words, his whole point of focus is to come here and to teach you to be extraordinary; he already is. And it is not about him producing phenomena. If he told you he was going to send you runners, you are going to get them big time. It is not about him doing tricks in front of you; that is not what he is. Those are tools of an avatar that is still a guru that needs to be worshiped, and that is not the case with him.

So what will happen is he will teach you and cultivate you and allow you to create the phenomenon, and you will be able to do that. And then one day when you are able to manifest on cue and you are able to leave your body and you are able to love, when it is to the human interest impossible to do that, one day he will walk right out here in your life because you are ready to share what he is. And what he is is simply what you are going to become. And until then he is diligent, patient, all-knowing, and all-understanding of everything that we need to know in order to learn to be that.

And the one thing I can say to you is that if you are interested in what you have heard in his presentation, and you are starting to love him even though you can't see him, that is a good sign because it means that what was

16

important in you was your soul urging you to unfold in this lifetime. And it may be against your neuronet. Your personality can argue with you and debate with you, but you are going to learn that that sort of logic is really transparent when the soul urges you onto an experience.

And I can just say that if this is what you want to do, you are going to have to exercise patience and focus and you are going to have to do the work. And the work in the beginning is very hard. But if you have the tenacity to stay with it, then one day I can tell you that this teacher is going to turn you inside out. And one day you will be able to do all the remarkable things that in myth and legend that the masters that you have heard of have the capacity to do. You will be able to do them because that is the journey. And ultimately that ability is singularly the reality of a God awakening in human form.

Now that is my journey and it has been my journey all of my life. And if it wasn't important and if it wasn't what it was, I certainly wouldn't be living in oblivion most of the year for the sake of having a few people come and have a New Age experience. This is far greater than a New Age experience. And I should also say that it is far more important than the ability to meditate or the ability to do yoga. It is about changing consciousness all through our lives on every point and to be able to unhinge and unlimit our minds so that we can be all we can be.

You should also know that what I have learned is we can only demonstrate what we are capable of demonstrating. And if you would say, well, what is blocking me from doing that, the only block that we have is our lack to surrender, our ability to surrender, our ability to allow, and our ability to support ourself even in the face of our own neurological or neuronet doubt. If you can support yourself through doubt, then you will make the breakthrough because that is the only block that stands in your way. And one day you are going to do all these things and get to see all the things that I have seen and been allowed to see.

So I just wanted to come out here and show you that I exist and that I love what I do and that I hope that you are learning from this teacher and, more importantly, I hope you continue with it.

— JZ Knight

THE ART OF PROPHECY

Greetings, my beloved masters. Let's have a drink.

O my beloved God —
O my beloved God —
hail unto you.
This that I be,
that I have called self,
allow it to transmute.
It is written,
ask unto that which you be
and it shall come forth.
O my God,
search my being;
search my sincerity.
Take away
that which is gray.
Fill me with passion.
Fill me with tolerance.
Fill me with strength.
Fill me with that which is termed allowance.
Burnish me impeccable
that, O my God,
what see you in I
will be worthy
of transmutation.
I desire it
from the Lord God of my being.
So be it.
To life.

If the only thing you ever asked for, in the simplest terms, spoken with understanding, were those words, you would find the kingdom of heaven. Be seated.

It is wonderful to see your numbers assembled. Are you here to learn? Are you panicked? Are you worried? Are you stressed? Are you ashamed? Are you happy? Well, there is no thing wrong with saying yea to any of the abovespoken. Now I am very pleased to see you.

Now there are those of you in this audience — Master Bonecracker and his beauteous woman — that have been in this audience nigh almost at the very beginning, and you have been steadfast. Now in these days do the events, as they are so termed, bring back those moments so long ago that were spoken of? Yes. You are living in fantastic times, fantastic indeed, for what seems worrisome and troublesome in the world as you so term it is the beginning of cataclysmic change for the whole dimension of this reality, as you term life, and nigh it will not cease for ten years.[1]

Prophecy, know you that term? What do you find prophecy to be in your language, eh? Prophets, as you may or may not know, in antiquity were highly revered entities. As a matter of fact, for your knowledge, they studied to be prophets. You know, like those of you who study to be lawyers, study to be physicians, they studied the art of prophecy. You can see that even in these times there are a few desperately needed ones. Unfortunately, prophets are no longer revered in the world because narrow-mindedness and consciousness has been given to the people generation upon generation, that that which controls their life is not choices but the destiny of impoverished stagnation of social life. There is no room to be a prophet. There is no room in the grid, as it were, to know truth.

That is perhaps why, so long ago in the audience, that many things that I gave openly to you were dismissed, excused, and even jested about. The irony is, of course, that none of you had the consciousness at that point completely to comprehend truth in a futuristic setting, nor did you have the ability to know, nor did you have the ability to have steadfast strength, tolerance, nor did you have the ability to rapidly change.

---

1 Notice this teaching was delivered on February 6, 1991.

Prophecy, as it were, has always been necessary, that a few great entities possess the ability, that they often have been the turning point in whole masses of humanity throughout history. If it were not for them, where you are today more than likely would not be here. And then it is the reverse: Because of them, you are precisely where you are today.

Now do you not find that to be an irony, that one should want to know so desperately what is to become of their life, but when you address it — an individual life and their turn of existence, who they are going to marry, what career should they take — such meaningless answers. So when you address it to the whole of humanity, realizing that every human being adds to the glory or the damnation of society as a whole, when you address them as a collective, they do not have the comprehension to understand. Yet they have asked for personal direction. There is no greater personal direction than to understand what you have not been. There is no greater imperative than to understand that in order to become that which is saintly, that which is masterful, and indeed that which is Christlike, that one must have the ability to change, to lay down that which was the past, to take up a garment that is unblemished, and the garment represents attitude.

There is no greater imperative than to know about your future, but not in very minute terms of social improvement or romance, as it is termed, but rather life, the answers. Many of you should recall, as it were, that many broad-spectrum prophecies were given to you as they were seen in that moment. Some of those prophecies have changed due to a great amount of intervention. Some are steadfast and must run their course in destiny, for nature is becoming intolerable of human waste, not only to that which is excreted from the body but the human waste of willingness, effort, and the imperative of being one with it.

All of this that was given — Jehovah and the great host, the dragons, indeed that which is termed twelve days of

23

light and the great battle to light up the Void like ten thousand suns, the government and the great world order — do these things sound familiar now? They were not familiar when I told you. They were excusable, unreal, fantastic — precisely. A society of human beings just like yourself, who want so desperately to have the miraculous, indeed to have the healing touch, indeed to have the wisdom of Solomon, indeed to have the mind of genius, that is what you want. But those in their sum total exist in a fantastic reality alongside with the prophecies. When you come into brilliance, enlightenment, knowingness, you see all as it really is and reject nothing, for nothing do you want hidden from you lest it become the shadow that taunt you or perhaps destroy you.

I gave you a great deal, indeed, of information. And it is to be certain that my language was not always understandable, and that became an excuse. I saw my words, as you term, edited and transposed for the sake of continuity of thought, and yet when the words were edited for the sake of continuity of thought, the words that were left out were words of profound power: "Indeed, as it were, in this time as you know it, unto this very hour, that which is termed, as it were indeed, the God within you, rise up, as it is so seen at this moment, to address that which is termed, as it were indeed, the deepening shadow that lies deep within the soul of that which is termed you and indeed all of that which is called humanity." Remember those words? They were left out for the sake of continuity. Now the words were powerful because they were not mere words. They were arranged according to the address, and the impact of their energy, and how they would be destined to bloom. So words that I have used in your past were there deliberately for the empowerment of the moment. I was the one delivering them; therefore I was obligated to bring them into being.

I have learned, as it is so termed, that for the sake of continuity, for the sake to continue to allow you to hear with no excuses, I banished the words of power, picked up indeed your language and your mimics, in order to teach you. The words are not as powerful, but at least the understanding is starting to come.

Now also when I did this, I also put away prophecy, for prophecy was only motivating a few in the name of fear, not knowledge or self-preservation. And it sent many away, running to their gurus, their priests, their teachers, their seers, their guides, their crystals — oh, God, what else; I am certain I have left out a host — for them to tell them 'tis not so, and taking great solace and comfort in saying that I had left. I never left.

It was time to set the record straight. It was written, edited, without the power, and no one wanted to know about destiny, save in that which is termed their personal life: Am I going to live? Will I get married? Where should I move? Where should I drill my wells for water? What should I eat? What should I wear? How should I talk? What should I do? Where should I live? They are meaningless questions.

So came understanding. In order for you to understand destiny, you had to come to a great amount of knowledge. How many words have we spoken together since the school of initiates began? How many terms have been pulled out of the intellectual mind to ascribe processes that are fantastic and as unreal as the dragon and Jehovah's host, or the plagues, or the One World Order? So many words to acclimate you to move freely to another consciousness, that all the terrible things that I have told you in the past, that you could begin to see them not as terrible any longer and not as fearful but see them from the prospect of a strengthened rather than impoverished mind, and even understanding the concept of mind and its reality, to give you the ability to know which way the wind is blowing, to have the sense of animals, simple as they are.

So that is where you are at. You have not gained the mastery of destiny because you are still as a collective fearful. You are still as a collective weak in many areas of understanding. That is not to make you feel ashamed, which is your next reaction. That is unnecessary. It is a truth in which one builds. It is a foundation in which one builds a great hovel on, which one builds a great consciousness on. You are not ready to understand further many more things that are yet shadows. They are unspoken of but they are getting ready to appear because you have not secured your fortress, preserved your life to where the security of what you are is untarnished.

So why did I, as you would term a prophet, tell you all of those horrible things? To wake you up, to make you aware. You cannot have superconsciousness without knowing about an alien host. If you can accept that, then you can accept superconsciousness. If you can accept the betrayal of governments, you can accept superconsciousness. If you can accept the reality and the validity of the plagues, you can accept personal healing. If you can understand the prejudice and bigotry that exist, then you can accept love and tolerance; to get you ready. It is all coming to pass and unfolding in dynamic measure. You are not being told the truth, as usual; you never have been. But there is much more coming now, which brings me to why so many of you are gathered here this night and felt compelled to be here.

WHY TEACH YOU THESE THINGS?
TO FIRE A NEW CONSCIOUSNESS IN YOU

So why am I teaching you all of these things? Indeed why teach you consciousness and energy, an intangible theory? Why teach you ultraviolet healing? Why teach you to see without eyes and to know without ears? Why teach you all of these things? Because if one is to exist in destiny — listen carefully — and if one is to exist in a superrace — meaning a race that has qualities I will discuss a wee bit later — if you are to exist beyond terrible times, you must prepare to live through those times not only as a physical creature who must feed and clothe and water the body beautiful but as a conscious being, the self.

Self is not the image in the mirror; it is what projects the image in the mirror, that self is prepared. To simply dig a hole and to bury foodstuffs will not be enough. But for one who resorts to the cave, the subterranean cave, with a powerful strength and consciousness, with proper training, one will be able to sustain through tremors, through upheavals of the likes you have never known, and in the midst of chaos, and buried beneath it all, find a steadfast focus, develop a greater knowingness to be able to see what occurs, to give inner strength to self — not the body, to consciousness — to be able to reach beyond the thickening veil of a rebirthing lifeform. Then we have a person who is preservable. We have an entity worthy of a new dawn. We have an entity worthy of the mastership of collapsing time. We have an entity worthy to walk on soil purified by fire and bring back life. We have an entity then worthy to travel through the Void and through space. I have a whole legion that will come and take you on such journeys.

But what can enter into kingdoms that I know? Let me tell you what can only enter therein. Warmongers and tyrants cannot enter where I talk about. Unimpeccable humans cannot enter. Those riddled with hatred and their garments spotted from their past cannot go. Those whose thoughts are profane, those whose thoughts turn to murderous rage and envy and jealousy and all of the things that have been conspired genetically to make you a slave race of people, you cannot go there, for those who will rest amongst the stars must be as indeed little children — little children not in the sense of ignorance but children in the sense of seeing all as a one and yet seeing the individual without judgment, and learning to love, because love is in the child, that which it seeks — a mind that is uncorrupted, ready for knowledge, a gentleness towered by strength, which means that in order to go to remarkable places from whence I know, one would be prepared to go if one, as it were, in the preparations for these times, as it were, were prepared passionately in consciousness as well.

And there is, as it is so termed, a trick to it all: Get rid of your past. Learn to have thoughts that are not based on the actions of yesterday. Indeed you have a savage in you, as it were, and a corruptible one, one that has been carefully manipulated and designed to be ignorant, to be hardworking, to be intolerant, and to possess hatred. That makes you a great army for war and social disorder.

All that you have called you is not the great self or God. It is a declaration of an image that you have lived. That is not to say that your parents are not real, and indeed your brethren are not real, indeed that your sistren are not real, that your children are not real. They are all real, but what has bound yourself through the image to them and all others has been your experiences of the past together based on memory. You are going to have to rise above to accept a greater thought, thoughts that come together and create echoes that cluster and form thoughtfulness, that thoughtfulness forms comprehension, and that comprehension forms a new knowledge. In other words, see yourself covered, as it were, in cow dung, dirt, and sweat from the toil in the field. Then see yourself bathed in clean water, washed and scrubbed, that the beauty of translucent and mahogany and jasmine faces comes shining through in an unearthly healthiness. That is what you must do with that which is termed your past. It must be washed away.

This trick throughout that which is termed your schooling I have been subtly teaching to you — sometimes very harshly, other times very quietly — to get you to change, stop being a victim. Victims die; they create disease in their bodies. When the body dies, so does the consciousness collapsing with it. That is called body/mind consciousness. It goes too, so very little substance is left of self, the evolving being.

And that is where you are at, at the present. You know very little about death. I shall engage you this evening to help you to understand that better, since there is a fear now rippling through many of you about dying. You are going to need the knowledge, for those of you who eventually choose the experience.

Then there are those of you who are scrubbing and you are cleaning, and I adore you to the depths of your beginnings. I understand your hardships, but I have seen you address them with the following criteria: You have not hidden them; you have allowed them to manifest. When there was fear and insecurity, you felt them but you turned to the one tool that you have learned and began to depend upon, the power of will, the breath, consciousness, and the beautiful Void. I have seen you in great passion, through the stimulus of fear and insecurity, turn that emotion into will. You marched into it like a great soldier.

Now many can criticize you, and have, about your foolish things that you do. A weak person will listen to the voices of the past and tradition, the wailing of the grid, and will succumb or hide away the problem. But a few of you — and your numbers are growing — have taken it not as a problem but as an opportunity to fire a new consciousness in you. Don't you understand that indeed, my beloved people, that what has motivated you and indeed created the destiny up to this point has been the memories and action/reaction of all of the past that you have ever lived continuing on? Your past has dictated your well-beingness or your insecurity or your pain and suffering. That has been how you define the things in your life.

Now those of you who took them on are now defining a higher calling, indeed a higher reason, a higher authority. Every moment that you take it on and apply what you have learned, you are building and integrating into self-present a greater consciousness that can be called a superconsciousness, bits and pieces. And the more that you address the hidden shame, the hidden guilt, indeed the hidden insecurity and go after it, the more that you do that and transmute it, the greater this consciousness grows.

Remember that the God of your being is likened unto a child that is just being born, and not yet born in some of you. It means that it must be fed and nurtured, which translates in your language to the understanding that you must apply the knowledge that you are gaining in this school, thereby taking the old and applying that which is termed the power of this truth to transmute it, that it is no longer an experience of the past and yet a new reality begins to form. You are feeding your God. It will one day be full-grown. It will have power and dominion over all matter.

And I have watched you very carefully. When others would think that you are having a hard time, I will look at you and say you are having a jolly wonderful opportunity. What are you made out of? What is the stuff of your being? How willful, indeed how strong are you? What have you learned? Is this greater than you or is it simply an echo of yesterday that keeps repeating itself?

To be a Christlike entity is magic, and yet the labor involved to hold such magic must mean literally the mastery of yesterday, the mastery of dualism, indeed the mastery of the impoverished, narrow-minded, body/mind consciousness that has been your inheritance in this generation. You cannot simply walk as a Christ; you must mature into one. Surely as you put bread and water and honey and wine on your tongue to give sustenance, sweetness, and flavor to your life, you must put equally amount in consciousness. You must take the bread of life, which is the Void, make it open to you; enter therein. You have to take the honey of self-choice and the wine of will to intoxicate you to change. What you put in your mouth must be equal to what you develop your mind with. Then we have got an initiate. Then indeed we have a master in the making. We have a glorious person blooming. We have an original being. Everything that comes your way these days is an opportunity to change. Indeed everything that comes your way emotionally is a runner from the past. It is your opportunity to own it once and for all as wisdom and engage a dynamic consciousness that can do the miraculous.

Then there are those of you who don't want to know, who do not want to hear because you are afraid you may have to change; you may have to do. You may have to be kind when you really want to hate. You may have to be tolerant when you really want to be intolerant. You may have to change your life completely. What your body cries out for because you addicted it, you are going to have to change and empower, to remove the addiction. You don't want to hear because you don't want to do that either. You are the ones that are either going to have to find a lost passion, or no matter how deep your hole, how great your food, when your past is shattered and the sun is no more and the earth trembles and is beaten down, you who have been weak to the past and weak to fear and insecurity and guilt and shame will not be able to live through what one who is mastering the past in a new criteria of knowledge will be able to withstand.

So where does your shame come from? Where does your guilt come from? Do you not know that fear is the catalyst to stress, and stress is the catalyst to that which is termed anxiety, and those are the catalyst for a body diseased, for a body dying? Where does that come from? What are you ashamed of? What are you guilty about?

These are all of the emotions that make your ears stop listening and make your eyes stop seeing, that forbid you to go to the Void, that do away with the passion for liberation and salvation. My beautiful people, these are the emotions that you call you. You will say, "That is me. That is how I feel" — I feel. "That is me, my persona."

What if all of you in this room no longer had any of those emotions? How would you then define yourself on a daily basis? How would you do it? What would your life be like? Are you listening? Well, a life lived without all of those emotions is simply the transference of energy from those into the revolution of joy. Then you have a God Almighty wise entity who knows and acts according to his or her knowingness, who never speaks a word unless the word has its manifested thought, that it is a word that is alive, pregnant with meaning and expression. You would see joy and would know for the first time unlimited freedom, not freedom from the work you are doing, no, but freedom from the stress, the shame, the guilt, the anxiety, and the insecurity about doing the work. That is what you are learning to do.

Now does that mean you must change and be a whole new person? It means you get clean. It means you cannot be in bondage by past attitudes and you cannot be in bondage by your body, in which you made the body your slave, and it you. It means a liberation. And now that is going to take work, isn't it? It is going to take work in being aware and indeed conscious. You are getting much too powerful to speak unconsciously. You are getting much too powerful to speak in anger and in bitterness and in treason. You are getting too powerful, as it were, to fabricate and to create rumors, because the rumors you create just might happen to you.

REMOVING THE BLOCKS
THAT PREVENT US FROM THE UNSEEN

Now what does this little talk have to do about prophecy? A great deal if you have been listening carefully, because straightaway you can understand now of why prophecy could never really be heard by you and understood by you, and why it struck fear in your soul, and why it caused you anxiety and heads that ache, because you are an emotional being that has been narrowly defined. What other way could you see it? Furthermore, how could you in yourself ever be a prophet? What would you be able to prophesize that was not based on fear and guilt and shame? Do you get it?

I want you to come to an understanding in this school, and subtly I am endeavoring to lead you there, to where you have the capacity to know awesome things without being a prophet, that you have the capacity to be so alert to such subtle changes in frequency you could determine them, and the moment you can determine them, the veil comes down from the dimensions, and what you determine must become reality. The reason that you do not have interplay with multiple dimensions at present: because you are a body/mind conscious being that is in the process of becoming a conscious-mind/body being. But the moment you begin to ascertain subtle changes in frequency, the reality of the unseen will be seeable by you. You will be able to look up here and to see me. I am standing, as you would term it, right here before you. I have always been standing here before you. The gold that you sometimes see, the light that moves off and around this body, is me.

Now you can only arrive there if what you are going to see is not predetermined by your past — do you understand? — because as long as it is, you are not going to see anything; I would make certain of it. Why? Because I do not want you to see into another dimension with a mind-set of yesterday, for example: to look upon a beauteous being and lust for them because that is your mind-set, it is your body-set; to look upon that which is termed a golden light and want to procure it for the sake of financial freedom; to look upon entities that don't quite look like you and to be prejudiced against them or judge them — they are ugly; beauty is an unseen essence, has nothing to do with physical members or apparatuses — or to make war, or to bargain with. You see? So, therefore, with a past consciousness you are locked out of a great reality for your own good.

Now if you are beginning to understand this, you are going to understand why also little have I said to you about further future events. It is enough — it is enough — that you begin to mold and grow a superconsciousness to be able to provide for yourselves, to preserve yourselves. There are those of you in this audience that have not nigh lifted a finger in that direction because you think I am lying to you. We will see. It is only an excuse.

Now I have taught you things that I knew, that I understood and I experienced. You will find fragments of perhaps those teachings in various places, but not all together. They are mythological terms; they are metaphysical terms. I am teaching you by laying down for you footprints that will take you somewhere forever. The things that I am teaching you may be bizarre — be prepared, be ready to move — but in order to do that, you must have the capacity for change, and if that is not in your past, how can you possibly do that? Be aware, which means simply to be conscious. Apply will. What do you do when you have none? You learn Consciousness & Energy[SM]. Be strong. Engagement of strength is often walking away. And being loving should be a goal sought by all of you. To love self does not mean, of past regards, to love your body. It means to love self, I Am, and that is a consciousness.

So how do you intercourse a consciousness? How do you dress it up? How do you take it out? How do you give it floras? How do you give it sweetmeats? Loving yourself has nothing to do with intercoursing the body. It has everything to do with wanting to be it completely, a lover to a lover. Being it completely means to purify it, to fall in love with it, to find love. When it is determined in self, then it can be determined to others. And what does that mean? To love self is to develop a new consciousness, that the past simply rolls up and becomes an experience in valuable proportions. But before it has done so, it is addressed and all of its restlessness is gleaned and addressed and mastered. Loving self is to stop thinking bad thoughts. Bad is your word; you understand that definition — bad, ugly, demeaning, profane, debauchery, envy, jealousy, intolerance. To love yourself is to wake up and say, "No more." And what you have been intolerant of, engage till you find it tolerant. And what you have hated and despised, engage it until you have found its beauty and love it so. And all of these things, in the end you will find were all of the aspects of you. That is the love of self.

Now we have a consciousness that cannot be held back. It is not worthy of sin; it is not worthy of salvation. It is its salvation. It is its eternalness. It will never die because it is no longer narrow-minded, nor is it mediocre, nor is it not worth preserving. It is sublime. The consciousness that exists in greater realities — in other worlds, in the depth of the Void, and indeed in the depths of space — that is the consciousness you got to walk in with.

So what is worth the loss here? To resign yourself in a very lazy and lethargic manner of not doing anything about your attitude, or waking up one fine morn and saying, "Alas, these teachings must become the fire of my truth"? And you must engage them till worthiness and pure you are to yourself. Then you are worthy for all eternity. Is it worth losing infinitesimal realities? Is it worth losing the power to heal in a touch, the magic to manifest? Is it worth losing the opportunity to see into worlds and realities unknown? Is it worth losing your life for?

Change to me came very painfully. That is perhaps why I don't have so much sorrowfulness for you who have problems, because when you see them as problems and hardship, I see them as a sword being run through you, and I know what happens. I know the healing, the agony, and the memory. But it took that to open me up to become conscious. The pain was so terrible that I could not sleep or lie down; I had to sit up for seven years. When you have to be aware because pain is making you aware, you change. Did I regret my past? No. Did I remember my past? No. It just was. You are going to have pain and suffering. You already have had. But when you decide that that is not awful but rather a fire of purification, it will pain you so that it may be the catalyst to eternity. To look for a life that is soft and comfortable, that is undemanding, is to look for a life of death. So what in your life is not an opportunity in these teachings to become greater? What have you lived through recently? How did you decide upon it? Did you accept it, bury it, or bring it on?

Now, my people, we are at that which is termed, as you call them, milestones in your learning. Appropriate night for this speech to an august body, because many of you in this audience are being spurred by fear, guilt, and shame, and you are suffering anxiety, and you are spreading rumors. And all of the energy that could have gone on to make it all happen for you, you have wasted in other areas. That is so like you from yesterday's imagery.

You have a lot more to learn. You have a lot more to experience, but if you are finding that Consciousness & Energy^{SM} is becoming boring to you, you have lost the meaning of why it is there, which means your grid has reached out and swallowed you up again. If you have lost the magic of manifestation, of healing, it is because you are back in the emotional turmoil that has kept you from the miraculous all this time. If you are ashamed that you do not do the discipline, it only means that you didn't want to do it, for shame would never have been an issue with desire — never was. And that was never an issue with learning. So if you are feeling ashamed of yourself because you haven't put it to use, it means you didn't want to — simple, bottom-line term — and if you didn't want to, I would rather you acknowledge that you do not want anything to happen, other than what is happening, than to honey-coat it with shame, because it is unnecessary. Be real. But I say to you, you have learned the magic of Gods. If you do not apply it, then self-worthiness cannot even be argued because you have not reached the garment of a God in order to even turn back. I tell you, you have learned a knowledge that the whole world should have learned, that it should have learned ages ago. You are behind nature in evolution. Is it any wonder that the events that are about to occur must occur?

Learn to Discern Thoughts That Come to You

There are healers in this audience that have not lifted a finger to help those who are desperately ill. What happens to a person who is desperately ill in this audience? Why cannot they heal themselves? I will tell you why. They have not broken the wave in consciousness to truly learn the passion, for their body consumes their strength because they have been nothing more than body/mind consciousness. But they are your brethren and your sistren. Why is it your obligation? It isn't, but for those who are learning love, who are finding those that they can exercise that love in a passion with a beginning learning only, it works wonders for both. Love is the greatest healer there is. Ultraviolet light only exists because love gave it birth.

There are entities in this audience that are doing all that they have the capacity to do to help themselves, and yet they need more help. There are those of you who have felt their thoughts and their callings, felt compelled by thinking of them out of nowhere, or thinking you should drop by, as it is so termed, but you negated the thought. They were calling for help. Learn to discern thoughts that come to you. Investigate them. That is the subtle communication that you will desperately need in the days to come. And what are you afraid of, that they will say, "No, I wasn't thinking about you"? Oh, what would you feel then? Embarrassed. Why should you be embarrassed? Is not embarrassment the same term as shame? What is there to be embarrassed or ashamed by? Love should never apologize for its actions. And if there is love there, there is no embarrassment. The truth is you haven't learned about love because you are still trying to figure out which one of you is doing what: "What is the image consciousness and what is the God consciousness, and since I cannot reach out and touch it, which is it, image or God?" You are still working through that. But every little thing helps.

Importance of Self-Forgiveness for Lucid Awareness

Now are you listening? Now here is something about your past you should know in regard to God, that force that is all in levels of manifested form and thought — God. Did you not know that the reason that religious sciences have been so successful is because in man's feeble understanding of the Gods and to keep hold of their robes, lest they leave, that the priests who speak in the name of God had the power and authority to forgive you? How important was that? I want you to listen. The reason that Christianity has bloomed so beautifully is because the underlying theme is forgiveness and salvation. God could forgive you of everything, and that gave you a new life. And you had to always pray that he would continue to forgive you of all the things you did daily wrong, which the prayer, of course, never ends.

But, masters, listen to me. So how important has it always been to be forgiven? The ultimate rejection of anyone is not to be forgiven by God, but the ultimate freedom, the ultimate joy, the ultimate bliss is to know that you asked God to forgive you of your misconduct, your impoverished thoughts, to forgive you of your sins, and through the name of Jesus Christ it was forgiven and you were saved. But what were you saved from? You were saved from your past. The reason that religion flourishes is on this truth.

Now you are the same, except you have found no one to forgive you of your misconduct, so you have had to suffer guilt, shame, embarrassment, and these have caused a great amount of anxiety, have enhanced your habits, and have put you on a life's road that is not altogether joyful.

I have masters in this audience who need to be forgiven. I forgive you. It is all forgiven. Now what have I forgiven you of? Now let me define this very important statement. Many of the reasons that you hold on to yesterday is because you have not been forgiven for it. That in turn makes you not worthy. And if not-worthiness is in you, you will have never made it to the Void, or across the field, or to your blessed name, because it is the underminer. It is the trap of the past.

Now if I forgive you of your past — which I ask your forgiveness for using such terms in a sentence — if I forgive you of your past, then why haven't you done the same? Because it denotes that you have done something wrong? Well, wrong does exist in your past because in order to have guilt and shame and sorrow, you have had to have done something wrong. So you first have to forgive, that the emotions go away, that wrong disappears, and all that is left is an experience. Do you understand?

Now salvation, what does salvation mean? You are going to be saved; what does that mean? Are you going to be saved from life, from death, from hell, from the government, from Jehovah, from your wife, your husbandman? This is very important because in order to be saved into that nebulous area, you must first have forgiveness. Now let us take this through, because these are words that I am going to bring on you in manifested form. In order for us to go quicker to the next milestone, this past issue must be addressed.

Salvation: Let me tell you what salvation is. Salvation is a new birth. It is a birth in consciousness to the extraordinary. It is the fever that burns away yesterday, and when you wake up, you are anew. It is the cleansing in the pure water from labor in the field. It is a pure thought transformed from a decadent one. Salvation is simply this — and this is the truth — that when a greater consciousness and attitude is thus established, it can only be established if forgiveness is exercised and the past is rolled up. But the past cannot go away unless it is forgiven and addressed. Then it makes room for clarity of thought, strength, and action, a motivation driven from passion instead of dread and fear. It gives you lucid dreams. It gives you lucid understanding. It allows you to see what is going on around you every single moment. It allows you to commune with nature, to the animal, the tree, the bird. That is being born again; that which you are resembles not that which you were. And that which is established in a consciousness that is greater than the consciousness of the body will live forever — forever. And as it grows, it has the power and capacity to keep the body intact forever, to take it all the way home, back to Point Zero, or to manifest it in any frequency on any level, in any dimension, in any time warp. It is being done all the time. It is just you are the ones, the whole world are the ones, who do not have the ability.

Now but religion ends with salvation, because religion closes the door on the quest of excellence, of mind and temperament and body and form and thought. It closes the door on the exploration that exists beyond the golden tabernacle. It closes the door on individualism. It closes the door on the desire to supersede beyond rhetoric. Salvation must be God made within, and the boundaries of God do not exist, for they are without boundary. Therefore the golden tabernacle does not hold the truth because the truth is in all life and it is visible to anyone who would look upon it. Man deserves wings in flight. Man deserves the journey in space, to the voyage of ten thousand galaxies. Man and woman both deserve to explore the kingdom of God that is without boundary. That is the difference. But where does it start? With you, for if I did not make you make the effort, then you would be certainly less than the Gods and a mere mortal after all who is denied immortality by his own or her own choice.

I am telling you, people, you are going to see the miraculous. You are going to taste the wine of will. You are going to know truth. You are going to see spectacular things beyond the walls of the tabernacle. The blood of Christ flows in everyone's veins.

Now I will let you contemplate that for a moment.

That was a great investment in a moment. Feel better? Then why don't you do that when you get depressed, sad, sorrowful, tired, and pitiful? You see, you are given the medicine for great mental health and you don't even take it.

Now you will contemplate what I have — indeed, as it were, into this time as you term it to be in this time in your counting — I have given forth unto that which is termed the Lord God of your being, from the Lord God of my being, that which is termed the even and correct truths? Yes. Forgiveness — forgiveness — means redemption from one's past. That is very important and crucial to all of you. Now do you remember everything I have told you?

Now before I go on to the next issue, what I want you to do to keep this foremost, what I have discussed with you this evening, up here, that it does not slip away, I want you to find one who is sitting within your vicinity. I want you to give that which is termed an address to them about what I have discussed and taught you this evening, and then you are to listen to their address back to you. In other words, no one leaves here without hearing what the message was.[2]

---

2 Participate and articulate the teaching to the best of your ability, even when you may not have a partner to share.

WHAT IN US IS AFRAID OF DEATH AND DYING?

Now what about death? What think you of death — death? Are you afraid of it? All people are afraid of death. You have some understanding as to why? Well, there are those truths that say the fabulous belief and theory — and I hope to God it is correct, reincarnation — you know, that you have lived before. But who were you and what did you do? You don't have any memories. Every human being wants to live. Every human being, consciousness in mass, is only aware when it is in mass that it is unaware.

Now because self is defined in every life as to are you a man or a woman — indeed are you rich or are you poor, what color is your skin, whence come you, what is your creed, and what is your tradition, the haves and the have-nots — the human being only begins to remember life the moment that it is born and begins to be cognizant of bodily functions: the need to fulfill its aching belly, to relieve its bowels, to feel, to touch, to sleep, to move. So life begins to be defined through the senses of the human body. And then understanding comes through that which is termed the benevolence or the indifference of parents and their tradition, that always depends upon where you are born and what time, what part of the world, what color your skin is, all of those unimportant things that become so important. You only become aware through mass. It is the great entrapment and it is also the great liberator. But life and memories and a true carving out to define what you are happens through the body, and it becomes territorial. It feeds you data about the impervious world around you in which you live. It allows you to express if it tastes good or it tastes bad, if it is pleasing to the eye or it is displeasing, if it is rough to the touch or smooth as silk, if it burns or it freezes or it cuts. So reality is defined by the body; miraculous concept. So life to you has been bodily experiences because those experiences only exist in a time frame. Mass in evolution can only evolve in time.

So what are you? You are the sum total of a sensory organ's complex experiences that define life, combined with that which is termed the teaching of your parents' tradition, creed, religion, and the time you were born. So then life has already been predetermined genetically, tradition should never be broken, so one generation succeeding the other follows in the footprints of its past, and this is what you call life. Well, if life is so mapped out, and if it is conditioned only through mass, and if reality, as it were, is conditioned only through mass, then what, alas, is to be remembered? What can be remembered? Genetics remember because they evolve based on experience. But if the experience of the genetic being, which you are, has not changed in 35,000 years, what is there to remember?

Now you don't remember before you came in. How can you? If you come in from a no-time dimension, there is no memory in a no-time dimension because there is no past in a no-time dimension. So you come in with no memory, you become a biological being conditioned by your social environment, without changing, without evolving, without becoming spectacular, different, or indifferent, and you hold on to this life. And you dread dying. You are afraid of death because you cannot prove that you exist before, even though the desire to believe in the theory of reincarnation, the myth, the metaphysical belief, you want to believe in it. You would follow anyone, listen to anyone that had anything to say about the preexistence of your soul, or rather your consciousness. You have done this in the past; you still yearn for information. And yet you cannot prove that what they say is correct because you have no memory except their memories of what they told you your memories were, and that is recycled ignorance at its best.

Now if you truly had a memory coming in of who you were before, then living life would be vastly different than what it is today, and death would no longer be a fearful, dreadful thing, an ominous rider from the blackness. You fear death because you cannot prove you lived before, and if you cannot prove you have lived before, then death is going to mean an absolute. So you hold on to life, and the more you hold on to it, the more you live it through a bodily function as a sensory organ, rather than an intelligent being, something with an intelligence that has nothing to do with intellect but has to do with power and movement, a convergence, if you will, of a dynamic essence about you that is different than the norm. So people pray to God. They look for prophets and seers to try to tell them of their immortality, because it is inevitable: From whence they came do they return, and that goes for you too.

So what is death to a conscious person? To an unconscious person, I can tell you this: It is indoctrination carefully implanted, that the essence or the sum total of human experience, even though it has been reenacted millions upon millions of lifetimes, is given back to the image from whence it came in the process of going to the light. It is a stripping process of giving back, in a way, and therein lies the mystery of no memory. For people who believe they are going to heaven, they will go to heaven; for people who believe they go to hell, they will go to hell, but they will have no memory of it. They will only believe because the reality is there for them to experience, but the memory will be lost if they can return. That is an unconscious and superstitious person.

A conscious person carefully begins to analyze the circumstance that, make no matter, the past is no longer important. It is the absolute Now that is the importance. Consciousness training and learning comes from Point Zero, not from some vague, distant point called yesterday or another life. It starts Now. The conscious person wakes up and begins to ascertain what he is beyond mysticism, beyond that which is termed superstition and beyond religion, and begins to define and chronicle the essence of self.

Now all that you have learned, perhaps the most important thing that you have learned, is that you are consciousness and energy inextricably combined, and that you are not your body, even though to this point you have so been your body. And the body dying or suffering to the very end is what causes the cold sweat on the back of your neck or the tingling between your breasts or the churning inside of your gut, because it is the ending of you, which has been nothing more than a physical being. Of course that is terrifying.

The Bands As Cumulative Intelligence

But self, beginning to be learned as consciousness and energy, an imageless entity, a oneness entity that resides in matter but also has the capacity to be any and every thing else in matter as well, this entity called self — you — begins to differentiate, as it is termed, between consciousness and mass. There is a difference between you and your body. The body is an entity but it is not the self that inhabits it. So you begin to understand that if you are consciousness and energy and a thought cannot be destroyed — it can be echoed upon but it can never be destroyed — that if you are consciousness, and consciousness being a collective of thought, then your consciousness is only as great as the collective thought that makes it up. And if the collective thought that makes it up has to do with reality perceived through the senses in the human body, then death is a certainty to that consciousness.

However, if consciousness then can be broadened and widened with knowledge, understanding, and then the application of that knowledge in actuality called experience, then self begins to emerge from within to take on a dominance that is greater than the human frailty of mass, or flesh and blood. Now what that means is that consciousness in and of itself lives in, within, and around every human cell that composes what you have thought to be yourself. Every single atom has bands. Every single particle has bands. And if the atoms make up the molecules that have bands that in turn make up the matter that has a band, that in turn makes up the mass that is a band that is widely distributed through its own program of genetic intelligence, then that means that every particle that constitutes the living human organism is one massive set of bands.

Now I want you to visualize that for a moment, that the tip of your little finger, the nail, that you call this, find its sharpest, longest point, or the end of one of your hairs. All of the cells that constitute the tip of your fingernail or the tip of your hair are immersed in two sets of bands. That means that this whole body, by God, is alive. In order for a single cell to exist, it must be composed of living particum. And we define living particum as that which exists in mass from consciousness, meaning it has an energy field. Every particum, every subatomic particum, has its own energy field. Now in order for this whole body to exist, this body then is being held together by a consciousness, and the consciousness is predetermined in the bands.

FIG. 1: SEVEN LAYERS THAT MAKE UP PHYSICAL MASS

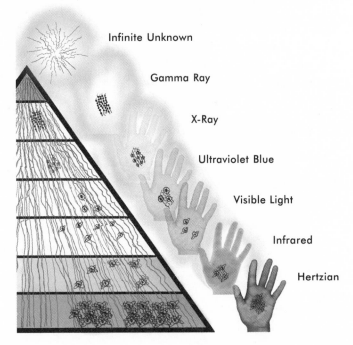

Infinite Unknown

Gamma Ray

X-Ray

Ultraviolet Blue

Visible Light

Infrared

Hertzian

FIG. 2: THE BANDS THAT HOLD THE BODY TOGETHER

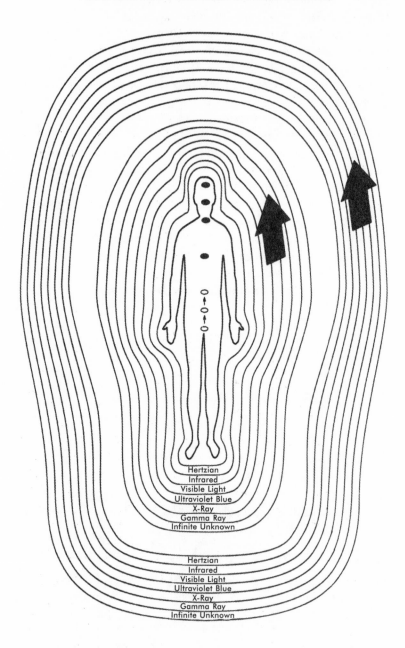

Hertzian
Infrared
Visible Light
Ultraviolet Blue
X-Ray
Gamma Ray
Infinite Unknown

Hertzian
Infrared
Visible Light
Ultraviolet Blue
X-Ray
Gamma Ray
Infinite Unknown

Now are you listening? That means that upon conception you as a consciousness were forming from your father's seed and your mother's egg, that it was your consciousness within the particums that constitute the genetic pattern that devised this entire organism. The sperm and the egg have their own life fields, but when they came together, the alchemy of that also created a new lifeform. So you are in a process of continuously coming in and out of life through the energy bands that surround mass or make mass possible.

So where were you before that? Can you really take you as you think you are, as bands, and somewhere isolate them from the oneness? Do you really think that because you are being developed in the womb of your mother that you have been isolated from the oneness? Is there a distance between you and your mother and the oneness? No, because the teaching is that everything is in the Now process, which means — I don't care if you lived 35,000 years ago and just now are unfolding like a budded lotus and getting ready to bloom — the difference between 35,000 years ago and this very moment has happened simultaneously, regardless of how much distance in linear time you would have had to travel to get to this point.

You Have Lived Numerous Lives
As Flowers on a Great Tree

Now contemplate this for a moment. You or your self is like the bud and the stem of a potential flower. The seed is planted in the ground and the sprout comes up. That means that you were the seed that went into fertile soil. But there is a blooming going to occur; that is the birthing of conscious self, the emergence from the womb. That is when the flower starts to bloom. In every life you have been the flowers on a magnificent bush or tree, and every lifetime is like a flower blooming. But when the flower wilts or is plucked and its life energy begins to diminish, where does the energy of the flower return to? The tree. So you have lived multitudinous lives symbolized as flowers on a great tree. This life is like a flower blooming, except you are a flesh-and-blood entity.

Now where is your consciousness then literally? Consciousness is within you. Consciousness lies within you literally because the potential for consciousness is the bands that surround every single particum that make up every single atom that make up every single molecule that make up every single cell that equates flesh in different design. You — you — your consciousness is defined by the bands swirling around the cells at the last of your hair. It is within you. It is not out there; it is in here. Now you are the flower connected to the great tree, but the great tree and the flower are one and the same.

So the consciously aware student begins to learn this, that there is no out-there path that one must travel to gain enlightenment or true realization. It is an inward understanding of the life force not being disconnected from the one, the tree. How many flowers have you been on this great tree of life, and where have you bloomed, what part of the tree? And you came back and you bloomed again, so you and the tree are one and the same because it is the tree that gave you life, but it was the flower and being the flower that gave you the power of individual expression. The bands that surround the human body are sort of like unto an aurora borealis. They are the outward bands that are made up of the great and many inward bands that constitute and contract to make mass. Remember, gross matter is a contraction of thought.

So if the student begins to understand that, then the student is freed from the fantasy of heaven and hell, and freed from the salvation of light, in knowledge of that that which constitutes self is made up in an electromagnetic spectrum of energy that collectively you have called your mind or your consciousness. Now if you can understand that and the moment that thought truly becomes aware to you within will begin to become so simple and obvious and clear that what retains itself after death and why it takes the physical body to move into the last throes or the instant cleft of dying, that the consciousness or what is termed the soul should be jarred loose, but only at those moments. What is being jarred loose is the first inward band closest to the human body, and that is consciousness and energy. When that moves away from the body, the body goes into a comatose state of unconsciousness, which means that the closest band to every single atom that constitutes your body has been moved from the focus of that point of matter.

Look at the bands. The one that is closest to your body, historically that has always been the band that has been called you in past lives, and it is that same band that has developed over lifetime over lifetime over lifetime in the same orderly, predictable fashion to bring forth a flower to bring forth color, to exhale perfume, intercourse, see the light, and go to sleep again. The band closest to your body could be defined as you because when it is closest to the body, it is the very band that holds all this together, and it is the representative of all those minute bands around all the atoms that make you up. Where else do you think consciousness and energy would reside? Do you really think that it would reside in some place outside of human understanding? It is the very crux of human understanding; furthermore, it is the very value that contracted to make the sperm and the egg and the new alchemy of a new self, a new flower.

Now so what is death? If consciousness is body/mind consciousness, it means that this band closest to the body has not evolved beyond the light or the image band. It is caught in the first three seals, in the first three levels of the spectrum. That means that you are your image, which translates to mean literally you are your body, conditioned by your past genetically. Now that has always pulled away, but what is death? Death is when that inward band moves away from the body. The body literally no longer has the intermediary of life force. In other words, it no longer has an image. It no longer has a conscious image, and that conscious image is carried down to the cells that are in the end of your fingernail. When that consciousness moves away from the body, the body has no other choice but to die. It has to, because it is that band that gives the body its function, its life, this treasure of awareness of the real world.

So the body dies when that moves away. What causes that to move away? Disease, pain, mental illness, which can be translated to say attitude. If you believe in the destiny of your unworthiness, death is your reward. If you believe in the attitudes of emotions that have ensnared you to the past, then death is your reward. You have set it up genetically, and you have set it up consciously, and you deteriorate. You fantasize about death; you are going to get it. You fantasized about killing someone; you will be killed. That is how you set it up in reality now, which means that if this band, the one closest to your body, refused to go anywhere, thus you have remarkable people who live to be one hundred and ten years old. That is remarkable in this time. If you have a willful entity who is willing life, who has arisen to the fact that it is beautiful, it is an oyster who has an enormous pearl that needs to be polished, then you have an entity who hangs in there and is going to live a very long time. But if you have one who has set up the program, consciousness moves out, immediately the body goes into a coma — immediately — because this band is the air in the lungs, it is the pounding of the heart, it is blood in the vein, it is a pulsating temple, it is watering eyes. So you are a within entity. The kingdom of heaven really is within you.

What Happens the Moment of Death?

Now so what happens to that person? Let me describe the scene to you. Hereto this person, let us say regardless of religious persuasion, has dreaded the moment of their death, has fought it like a true warrior, holding on to nothingness, has never experienced anything extraordinary because he was forbidden, she was forbidden. So this is a narrow, narrow-minded entity. So the moment comes. Things are getting foggier, thought is becoming more pronounced, but the room is getting hazy. And suddenly, in a moment, you don't feel like lying there any longer so you get up, get off of the pallet, you stand up, and you walk around, and you suddenly realize you feel wonderful: No more pain, no more sadness, you feel lighthearted and light-minded, and never was a moment so lucid. It must be those moments your grandmother told you about that every once in a while, when you got down to that which is termed the bottom of the bucket, it was at that moment you realized how full it was moments earlier, except you turn around and there is still someone laying on the pallet. And you look at it, and you look at it a little closer, and you walk over to it, and you look down into its face, and you put your finger through it, and you touch yourself and you are solid. Who is who? You can touch your wrist, your hair, your face. Why, you are even wearing the same garments you had on, and yet you didn't even know when it occurred. Why, it was really nothing. And suddenly you realize you have died, but that must be the worst joke anyone ever played on anyone, because for the first time in your life, you are out of your body, and yet you, self, is distinctly different than the body that is lying there, perhaps contorted in pain. You don't have any pain. You don't feel any heaviness. The room, as it were — and you begin to notice everything — takes on a sheen, perhaps best called iridescent sheen because it is like looking through a translucent pearl. But the irony is you have left something you always thought was yourself, but your self is still intact without it.

So how could your body feel so real, you know, the one that is feeling so good now? How could it be solid and you could put your hand through the body you just left? Which is the real world? Which is the real world? If you can put your hand through the dead body but you can pound it on your chest, now which one is real? What has happened to you? What has happened to you is that the first band has moved away or contracted from every single particle that constitutes the body, and it has moved out of the sphere of the bands. So the body you are now experiencing is a body that is made up of the light and infrared, and yet it is very solid because it is vibrating at a frequency that is a higher rate than the density of matter. And what that means is that every little particle that made up you, every one of those atoms, every one of those cells, you might as well have reached over and taken their first band out of every one of them, reconstructed it, and you have the same body, except it is vibrating at a different frequency, but it is solid.

Now the irony is that this body can see everybody else, but everybody else can't see this body seeing everybody else. Death is not a long night. It happens less than a twinkling of an eye. It is that moment on the edge of twilight, in the alpha state. It is that moment, the fluttering of eyelashes, weary and tired, fighting the pain or just plain exhausted. And it is that moment at twilight when the eyelashes flicker and the eyes close to rest, and you wake them back up, and everything is the same except for one distinct fact: You are no longer your body, and you are no longer subject to its pain, its suffering, its agony, its heaviness, its misery because the body you inhabit has pulled entirely away from mass.

Now various things happen to this entity, according to what level of consciousness they have been on. The body you are going to see them in is the body they always thought they were, and it stands to reason that the body existing in moments after death will be identical to the body that was left behind. After all, we are talking about body/mind consciousness. Various things happen to this wonderful entity. He can go to the light, to the artificial light, to where it is a trap, get stripped, have no remembrance whatsoever, even be stripped of his wonderful body, sent into a deep sleep only to return again, contracted into a new seed or the alchemy of the seed and the egg; or he can go to the everlasting light, the blending into the eternal Void, and there the journey is quite different. However, rarely do entities who are body/mind consciousness, even though death is a no-thing in the twinkling of an eye, ever get beyond the light. You know why? Because just like the body they inhabit presently, their consciousness is no greater to encompass the seascape of magnificent realities other than what it is used to.

WHEN OUR IDENTITY STRETCHES OUT FAR BEYOND OUR BODY

Now let us take perchance one of you, and in our sublime arrogance we are going to say you are a conscious entity and have understood that you are within, and that which constitutes your body is the consciousness that keeps it intact. And you have come to realize that and understand that if the body is the contraction of both of these bands, then what was the original Source and, my God, what did it look like? Well, let's presume for just a moment that you are not tired and weary, and that you really do want to be more than your body. Perhaps your identity is no longer constricted to that element, that it is as broad as the Void. Let's pretend.

First off, such a brazen and beautiful entity wouldn't even have the thought of dying, you see, because life now has much more to offer than simply the past and the image and making sure the body is taken care of, from its sexuality all the way to the last hair on its head, but life now is an adventure. My God, to realize that your consciousness is the function of every atom in your body is a miraculous thought, for that in itself is divinely beautiful because if you understood that that is exactly what you were, then in any moment after that understanding, you could direct your attention to any part of your body, spin those bands in any way that you wanted to, rotate them, reverse them, change radical cells that create cancer, and get them on the right path — and they would listen to you because, after all, they are you — to be able to go internally and clean it out, make it new, wash it inside out, and have life to discover, and journeys and places to go, and to try your best to raise its frequency, spinning those bands on every single molecule in your body to levitate it off of the floor — and, my God, who needs wings after that? — to do remote-view; in an instant the body manifests any way you want it to; to be young again; to be regally old and wise; to be anything: the adventure of mass, because it is God, is unlimited.

But if you ever decided you wanted to die, you could die. You could even determine the day and the time. You could make all of the arrangements, have all of the family and friends there, make sure everything is done right. And once everyone has shown up, had some wine, lots to eat, danced, visited, socialized, you could die and it would be all over. You simply lie down and go. Now for those of you who are that well, you are probably saying, "I don't want to take this body," so you lie it down, you get up, and you start a rainbow of transition. You walk out of the body as the body itself, the third and the second levels. And it is beautiful, and you are powerful, and you are wonderful, and you know it. You are light, airy, and free. Why, you could even jump and hit the ceiling and go through the next level. You could go up in front of Aunt Sarah's face and laugh at her. Imagine Aunt Sarah, tolerating her kidneys all these years. You could go and do anything you wanted to, and then you could go into the most beautiful lightbody ever. That is the level of the image; it is a beautiful and spectacular place. It is an unbelievable light that is more brilliant than anything you have ever known, but you can look at it because you are it. A being — imagine — you, robed in light, wonderful, powerful. At that moment you can change; why, you can change that dirty shirt for a clean white robe of light. You can make your hair grow long. You can look like Jesus, Aunt Sarah, or a butterfly. You can come back to all the places you lived, visit it in your lightbody. You can appear beside your relatives' bed, scare the hell out of them, answer some lost soul's prayer you happen to stumble across who only wants a vision, and in a moment you could become the vision and give them wise, wise words to follow. You can change lives and sink ships. That has a lot to offer. It is a wonderful place to go.

And then you can move from that lightbody to a radiant body. It is just on the other side of visible light. Now we are talking levels of movement within movement, prisms of color yet unseen and undefined, the ability to be the heat in an engine, the ability to be azure blue on a butterfly's wings, the ability to experience being a tear in a forgotten child's eyes, to be a warm wind to a lonely heart, to sail the seas of the Void to the heights and depths; to be with entities in other worlds and other realities, to sup with them, to dance with them, to laugh with them, to learn with them; to take on any body, put any body down; to move to the realms of a greater intelligence in consciousness; to be a moving ocean or a raging storm on any world, any level, and any place; to be someone's dream, their hope, to be their vision, to send them the thought of profoundly simple and inspiring words, and watch them utter them; to watch someone bloom and to grow; to utilize them to help others; to lay on a cloud on any world, any plane, and any level; to rest in the bosom of God; to suckle at the breast of what being alive was always about.

Depending on where you are when you decide to make this journey, and to what far reaches in consciousness you have been, how far you have stretched yourself, to what unlimited capacity and joy could you experience is equal to — and only to — the level in which you experience as a person who has passed this plane. You don't go any higher than what you are at the moment of departure. You can see everything below you, understand it perfectly; you can move mountains and sink ships, but to go beyond that point, you can go no further than what you are aware of. In other words, all the bodies that make you up are seven in number.

Death, it depends upon where you are at, indeed what you think. How great or how small your consciousness is how powerful death will be on you. In the twinkling of an eye, you are the same but different. But if you are locked in to this reality and you are body/mind consciousness, you will be tormented by this reality. People you love so much, or rather you possess so much, and they can't hear you, they can't forgive you, and you can't forgive them. People you want to embrace, you wished you would have;

you cannot embrace them. It is empty arms, only a cold breeze on a hot cheek. All the things you wished you would have done, you try to do but make no difference, because one who is bound into this reality is only as powerful as when he was alive.

There is no proof that you lived before for you. You will only have to take my word that you did. You are not an instantaneous creation. You are not the star floating on midnight blue in the alchemist's crucible. You didn't just occur; you have always been. You are just another flower at a different part on the tree, and perhaps in this life you are a little higher up on the upper branches because the warmth of love, symbolic of the sun, and the winds of change have been a part of this budding and this existence. The ground is a long, long way away.

Life in this body can be bliss or it can be the demons that torment you forever, till the day you die, but the consciousness that determines that reality is at this very moment giving succor, confidence, or denial through every single organism that makes up that body. When you decide to pull away, the condition of your mental health will be fairly obvious as to the condition of the human body when you pulled away.

You have within you and before you an eternal knowledge, one that not only engenders hope but that you don't have to go out and buy it or beg some priest's forgiveness or ask Christ to forgive you. Ask your Christ to forgive you. The hope is within you. God was never more the intake and exhale of every breath you ever took. God could never have been closer. How else could God have known the numbers of hairs on your head at this very moment? It could only know that because it is it. And the record of your body is locked up in those bands because without those bands, there wouldn't be a human body. Yes.

So this is good news. If you bite it, it won't hurt long. At least you know something now. I would suggest however that instead of contemplating dying in these terrible times, relish every moment of living. Now that is not an excuse to go out and be thunderously wrong, to do ill will, to cheat and rob, to transgress, to kill, to murder, to maim, to say hateful things. That is not living; that is dying. Grab ahold of yourself. Look at your hand before you slumber tonight, because what has made up this hand is what is going to survive its demise.[3] Perhaps one day you will stay around long enough to where you will look at this beautiful hand and take it back with you whence you go so that the great outer band that has to stay in place until its decay can be released as well. The outer band will stay with the body until it deteriorates, otherwise it could not have form. What a waste. The outer band is only released when the consciousness of the entity is beyond the consciousness of visible light in the spectrum. That is when bodies disappear, deteriorate, or go in the flame with the wind. But as long as consciousness is equal only to the image, the outer band stays as the life force or the guardian of the flesh until it is no more — ashes to ashes and dust to dust. You are not going to get a long ways as an awakened self with only one band. You will remain eternal in the Now if you have both of them.

Now you will understand indeed why love I you greatly and call your bodies beautiful when in your own eye you can never see them that way: They are never good enough; they are never young enough; they are never beautiful enough; they are never anything enough. Love them by loving yourself. They are God too. Otherwise they would not inherit the greatest band of them all, the outer band, to stay with it until it is no more.

I am going to send you runners in regard to all of the emotions we have discussed this evening, to understand true compassion and the keys of forgiveness and salvation and what that means. I want you to experience what I have rambled on here to you this evening. Furthermore, I want you to have a great sensation with your body, in particular a sensation of being more than your body. I desire the experience for the lot of you so that the fear of dying in a

3 See fig. 1 on p. 53.

69

time that seems to be most turbulent will have its case rested, and the business of being preservable and preserved for a greater time and a greater morn. You can go about your business with peace of mind, with joy, and you will get a lot more accomplished. And without this fear you will have the ability to learn great and wonderful things and will deserve the knowledge.

Now I want you — your time, twice — twice in one month I want you to give one item. It must begin with food, twice a month, one item of food, and the food shall go to a list of entities that are your brethren and sistren that have not had the courage in consciousness as of yet to manifest the food that needs so desperately to be stored. Very, very soon you will not be able to do this. Help one another. There are a thousand in number here this evening. If you gave but one item to someone, it would give them a thousand days of life. Twice in your months I want you to do this, not because you have to but because you want to. So be it.

Keep your eyes on the skies. You will see, in a fortnight, there will be a great amount of activity over North America. The green fireballs are coming back into your sphere; they are being sent as well as those that will appear orange. Keep your eyes aware in daytime, in particular in the afternoon at the time called two. There will be a great amount of activity all through to summer. If you look up, you may see them. You may see some spectacular ones, and they are not all bad.

If you must travel to the city, take your own water from your own wells with you. Do not drink the water in the cities. Your food is poisonous. Grow your own food. Learn to eat what comes from someone that you know. Do you understand? The plagues are reaching epic proportions. They are transmuting. I would advise you very strongly to stay as far from the cities as you can. They are not a terrible place but they are the breeding ground for a lot of death. And continue your labor, but do it in a great attitude. Do you hear me? Now last, love I you greatly.

There is great prophecy that can be told you, but none much more exquisite than what I told you this evening, for prophecy and world events, they are yesterday's news. They are unfolding as planned. But what you have been given is an opportunity for an eternal life, and it is close at hand. And it is not hard unless you don't want it; then it becomes hard.

The next time you are in this audience, don't engage Consciousness & Energy^{SM} because you have to but rather because the desire and passion is there. It is magic. It brings a great God from birth into adulthood. It can create miracles and warp reality and time. But it is only as strong as the pursuing attitude that is always there to undermine it. That is a body/mind consciousness attitude. You must be ever alert to that and continuously reinstate your power and your direction. Never take for granted that you are going to be all right — never.

This school will greatly grow this year in your time in counting, for those that left so long ago and in the near future are seeing what they once heard as fantastic coming to pass, so now they want to come back to the source. Maybe I have returned.

I love you, my beautiful people. It gladdens my being to have seen you here this evening. It gladdens my being to have simply talked to you this evening. It gladdens my being that I am God enough for you to still come and listen and learn.

— Ramtha

RAMTHA'S GLOSSARY

Analogical. Being analogical means living in the Now. It is the creative moment and is outside of time, the past, and the emotions.

Analogical mind. Analogical mind means one mind. It is the result of the alignment of primary consciousness and secondary consciousness, the Observer and the personality. The fourth, fifth, sixth, and seventh seals of the body are opened in this state of mind. The bands spin in opposite directions, like a wheel within a wheel, creating a powerful vortex that allows the thoughts held in the frontal lobe to coagulate and manifest.

Bands, the. The bands are the two sets of seven frequencies that surround the human body and hold it together. Each of the seven-frequency layers of each band corresponds to the seven seals of seven levels of consciousness in the human body. The bands are the auric field that allow the processes of binary and analogical mind.

Binary mind. This term means two minds. It is the mind produced by accessing the knowledge of the human personality and the physical body without accessing our deep subconscious mind. Binary mind relies solely on the knowledge, perception, and thought processes of the neocortex and the first three seals. The fourth, fifth, sixth, and seventh seals remain closed in this state of mind.

Blue Body^{SM}. It is the body that belongs to the fourth plane of existence, the bridge consciousness, and the ultraviolet frequency band. The Blue Body^{SM} is the lord over the lightbody and the physical plane.

Blue Body^{SM} Dance. It is a discipline taught by Ramtha in which the students lift their conscious awareness to the consciousness of the fourth plane. This discipline allows the Blue Body^{SM} to be accessed and the forth seal to be opened.

Blue Body^{SM} Healing. It is a discipline taught by Ramtha in which the students lift their conscious awareness to the consciousness of the fourth plane and the Blue Body^{SM} for the purpose of healing or changing the physical body.

Blue webs. The blue webs represent the basic structure at a subtle level of the physical body. It is the invisible skeletal structure of the physical realm vibrating at the level of ultraviolet frequency.

Body/mind consciousness. Body/mind consciousness is the consciousness that belongs to the physical plane and the human body.

Book of Life. Ramtha refers to the soul as the Book of Life, where the whole journey of involution and evolution of each individual is recorded in the form of wisdom.

C&E^{SM} = R. Consciousness and energy create the nature of reality.

C&E^{SM}. Abbreviation of Consciousness & Energy^{SM}. This is the trademark of the fundamental discipline of manifestation and the raising of consciousness taught in Ramtha's School of Enlightenment. Through this discipline the student learns to create an analogical state of mind, open up its higher seals, and create reality from the Void. A Beginning C&E^{SM} Workshop is the name of the introductory workshop for beginning students in which they learn the fundamental concepts and disciplines of Ramtha's teachings. The teachings of the Beginning C&E^{SM} Workshop can be found in *Ramtha, A Beginner's Guide to Creating Reality,* revised and expanded ed. (Yelm: JZK Publishing, a division of JZK, Inc., 2000), and in *Ramtha: Creating Personal Reality,* Video ed. (Yelm: JZK Publishing, a division of JZK, Inc., 1998).

Christ walk. The Christ walk is a discipline designed by Ramtha in which the student learns to walk very slowly and acutely aware. In this discipline the students learn to manifest, with each step they take, the mind of a Christ.

Consciousness. Consciousness is the child who was born from the Void's contemplation of itself. It is the essence and fabric of all being. Everything that exists originated in consciousness and manifested outwardly through its handmaiden energy. A stream of consciousness refers to the continuum of the mind of God.

Consciousness and energy. Consciousness and energy are the dynamic force of creation and are inextricably combined. Everything that exists originated in consciousness and manifested through the modulation of its energy impact into mass.

Disciplines of the Great Work. Ramtha's School of Ancient Wisdom is dedicated to the Great Work. The disciplines of the Great Work practiced in Ramtha's School of Enlightenment are all designed in their entirety by Ramtha. These practices are powerful initiations where the student has the opportunity to apply and experience firsthand the teachings of Ramtha.

Emotions. An emotion is the physical, biochemical effect of an experience. Emotions belong to the past, for they are the expression of experiences that are already known and mapped in the neuropathways of the brain.

Energy. Energy is the counterpart of consciousness. All consciousness carries with it a dynamic energy impact, radiation, or natural expression of itself. Likewise, all forms of energy carry with it a consciousness that defines it.

Enlightenment. Enlightenment is the full realization of the human person, the attainment of immortality, and unlimited mind. It is the result of raising the kundalini energy sitting at the base of the spine to the seventh seal that opens the dormant parts of the brain. When the energy penetrates the lower cerebellum and the midbrain, and the subconscious mind is opened, the individual experiences a blinding flash of light called enlightenment.

Evolution. Evolution is the journey back home from the slowest levels of frequency and mass to the highest levels of consciousness and Point Zero.

Fieldwork^{SM}. Fieldwork^{SM} is one of the fundamental disciplines of Ramtha's School of Enlightenment. The students are taught to create a symbol of something they want to know and experience and draw it on a paper card. These cards are placed with the blank side facing out on the fence rails of a large field. The students blindfold themselves and focus on their symbol, allowing their body to walk freely to find their card through the application of the law of consciousness and energy and analogical mind.

Fifth plane. The fifth plane of existence is the plane of superconsciousness and x-ray frequency. It is also known as the Golden Plane or paradise.

Fifth seal. The fifth seal is the center of our spiritual body that connects us to the fifth plane. This seal is associated with the thyroid gland and with speaking and living the truth without dualism.

First plane. It refers to the material or physical plane. It is the plane of the image consciousness and Hertzian frequency. It is the lowest and densest form of coagulated consciousness and energy.

First seal. The first seal is associated with the reproductive organs, sexuality, and survival.

First three seals. The first three seals are the seals of sexuality, survival, pain and suffering, victimization, and tyranny. These are the seals commonly at play in all of the complexities of the human drama.

Fourth plane. The fourth plane of existence is the realm of the bridge consciousness and ultraviolet frequency. This plane is described as the plane of Shiva, the destroyer of the old and creator of the new. In this plane, energy is not yet split into positive and negative charge. Any lasting changes or healing of the physical body must be changed first at the level of the fourth plane and the Blue Body^{SM}. This plane is also called the Blue Plane, or the plane of Shiva.

Fourth seal. The fourth seal is associated with unconditional love and the thymus gland. When this seal is activated, a hormone is released that maintains the body in perfect health and stops the aging process.

God. Ramtha's teachings are an exposition of the statement, "You are God." Humanity is described as the forgotten Gods. God is different from the Void. God is the point of awareness that sprang from the Void contemplating itself. It is consciousness and energy exploring and making known the unknown potentials of the Void. It is the omnipotent and omnipresent essence of all creation.

God within. It is the Observer, the true self, the primary consciousness, the Spirit, the God within the human person.

God/man. The full realization of a human being.

God/woman. The full realization of a human being.

Gods. The Gods are technologically advanced beings from other star systems that came to Earth 455,000 years ago. These Gods manipulated the human race genetically, mixing and modifying our DNA with theirs. They are responsible for the evolution of the neocortex and used the human race as a subdued work force. Evidence of these events is recorded in the Sumerian tablets and artifacts. This term is also used to describe the true identity of humanity, the forgotten Gods.

Golden body. It is the body that belongs to the fifth plane, superconsciousness, and x-ray frequency.

Great Work. The Great Work is the practical application of the teachings of the Schools of Ancient Wisdom. It refers to the disciplines by which the human person becomes enlightened and is transmuted into an immortal, divine being.

Hierophant. A hierophant is a master teacher who is able to manifest what they teach and initiate their students into such knowledge.

Hyperconsciousness. Hyperconsciousness is the consciousness of the sixth plane and gamma ray frequency.

Infinite Unknown. It is the frequency band of the seventh plane of existence and ultraconsciousness.

Involution. Involution is the journey from Point Zero and the seventh plane to the slowest and densest levels of frequency and mass.

JZ Knight. JZ Knight is the only person appointed by Ramtha to channel him. Ramtha refers to JZ as his beloved daughter. She was Ramaya, the eldest of the children given to Ramtha during his lifetime.

Kundalini. Kundalini energy is the life force of a person that descends from the higher seals to the base of the spine at puberty. It is a large packet of energy reserved for human evolution, commonly pictured as a coiled serpent that sits at the base of the spine. This energy is different from the energy coming out of the first three seals responsible for sexuality, pain and suffering, power, and victimization. It is commonly described as the sleeping serpent or the sleeping dragon. The journey of the kundalini energy to the crown of the head is called the journey of enlightenment. This journey takes place when this serpent wakes up and starts to split and dance around the spine, ionizing the spinal fluid and changing its molecular structure. This action causes the opening of the midbrain and the door to the subconscious mind.

Life force. The life force is the Father, the Spirit, the breath of life within the person that is the platform from which the person creates its illusions, imagination, and dreams.

Life review. It is the review of the previous incarnation that occurs when the person reaches the third plane after death. The person gets the opportunity to be the Observer, the actor, and the recipient of its own actions. The unresolved issues from that lifetime that emerge at the life review set the agenda for the next incarnation.

Light, the. The light refers to the third plane of existence.

Lightbody. It is the same as the radiant body. It is the body that belongs to the third plane of conscious awareness and the visible light frequency band.

List, the. The List is the discipline taught by Ramtha where the student gets to write a list of items they desire to know and experience and then learn to focus on it in an analogical state of consciousness. The List is the map used to design, change, and reprogram the neuronet of the person. It is the tool that helps to bring meaningful and lasting changes in the person and their reality.

Make known the unknown. This phrase expresses the original divine mandate given to the Source consciousness to manifest and bring to conscious awareness all of the infinite potentials of the Void. This statement represents the basic intent that inspires the dynamic process of evolution.

Mind. Mind is the product of streams of consciousness and energy acting on the brain creating thought forms, holographic segments, or neurosynaptic patterns called memory. The streams of consciousness and energy are what keep the brain alive. They are its power source. A person's ability to think is what gives them a mind.

Mind of God. The mind of God comprises the mind and wisdom of every lifeform that ever lived on any dimension, in any time, or that ever will live on any planet or any star.

Monkey-mind. Monkey-mind refers to the flickering mind of the personality.

Mother/Father Principle. It is the source of all life, God the Father, the eternal Mother, the Void.

Name-field. The name-field is the name of the large field where the discipline of Fieldwork^SM is practiced.

Observer. It refers to the Observer responsible for collapsing the particle/wave of quantum mechanics. It represents the true self, the Spirit, primary consciousness, the God within the human person.

Outrageous. Ramtha uses this word in a positive way to express something or someone who is extraordinary and unusual, unrestrained in action, and excessively bold or fierce.

People, places, things, times, and events. These are the main areas of human experience to which the personality is emotionally attached. These areas represent the past of the human person and constitute the content of the emotional body.

Plane of Bliss. It refers to the plane of rest where souls get to plan their next incarnations after their life reviews. It is also known as heaven and paradise where there is no suffering, no pain, no need or lack, and where every wish is immediately manifested.

Plane of demonstration. The physical plane is also called the plane of demonstration. It is the plane where the person has the opportunity to demonstrate its creative potentiality in mass and witness consciousness in material form in order to expand its emotional understanding.

Point Zero. It refers to the original point of awareness created by the Void through its act of contemplating itself. Point Zero is the original child of the Void.

Ram. Ram is a shorter version of the name Ramtha. Ramtha means the Father.

Ramaya. Ramtha refers to JZ Knight as his beloved daughter. She was Ramaya, the first one to become Ramtha's adopted child during his lifetime. Ramtha found Ramaya abandoned on the steppes of Russia. Many people gave their children to Ramtha during the march as a gesture of love and highest respect; these children were to be raised in the House of the Ram. His children grew to the great number of 133 even though he never had offspring of his own blood.

Ramtha (etymology). The name of Ramtha the Enlightened One, Lord of the Wind, means the Father. It also refers to the Ram who descended from the mountain on what is known as the Terrible Day of the Ram. "It is about that in all antiquity. And in ancient Egypt, there is an avenue dedicated to the Ram, the great conqueror. And they were wise enough to understand that whoever could walk down the avenue of the Ram could conquer the wind." The word Aram, the name of Noah's grandson, is formed from the Aramaic noun Araa — meaning earth, landmass — and the word Ramtha, meaning high. This Semitic name echoes Ramtha's descent from the high mountain, which began the great march.

Runner. A runner in Ramtha's lifetime was responsible for bringing specific messages or information. A master teacher has the ability to send runners to other people that manifest their words or intent in the form of an experience or an event.

Second plane. It is the plane of existence of social consciousness and the infrared frequency band. It is associated with pain and suffering. This plane is the negative polarity of the third plane of visible light frequency.

Second seal. This seal is the energy center of social consciousness and the infrared frequency band. It is associated with pain and suffering and is located in the lower abdominal area.

Self, the. The self is the true identity of the human person. It is the transcendental aspect of the person. It refers to the Observer, the primary consciousness.

Sending-and-receiving. Sending-and-receiving is the name of the discipline taught by Ramtha in which the student learns to access information using the faculties of the midbrain to the exclusion of sensory perception. This discipline develops the student's psychic ability of telepathy and divination.

Seven seals. The seven seals are powerful energy centers that constitute seven levels of consciousness in the human body. The bands are the way in which the physical body is held together according to these seals. In every human being there is energy spiraling out of the first three seals or centers. The energy pulsating out of the first three seals manifests itself respectively as sexuality, pain, or power. When the upper seals are unlocked, a higher level of awareness is activated.

Seventh plane. The seventh plane is the plane of ultraconsciousness and the Infinite Unknown frequency band. This plane is where the journey of involution began. This plane was created by Point Zero when it imitated the act of contemplation of the Void and the mirror or secondary consciousness was created. A plane of existence or dimension of space and time exists between two points of consciousness. All the other planes were created by slowing down the time and frequency band of the seventh plane.

Seventh seal. This seal is associated with the crown of the head, the pituitary gland, and the attainment of enlightenment.

Shiva. The Lord God Shiva represents the Lord of the Blue Plane and the Blue Body^SM. Shiva is not used in reference to a singular deity from Hinduism. It is rather the representation of a state of consciousness that belongs to the fourth plane, the ultraviolet frequency band, and the opening of the fourth seal. Shiva is neither male nor female. It is an androgynous being, for the energy of the fourth plane has not yet been split into positive and negative polarity. This is an important distinction from the traditional Hindu representation of Shiva as a male deity who has a wife. The tiger skin at its feet, the trident staff, and the sun and the moon at the level of the head represent the mastery of this body over the first three seals of consciousness. The kundalini energy is pictured as fiery energy shooting from the base of the spine through the head. This is another distinction from some Hindu representations of Shiva with the serpent energy coming out at the level of the fifth seal or throat. Another symbolic image of Shiva is the long threads of dark hair and an abundance of pearl necklaces, which represent its richness of experience owned into wisdom. The quiver and bow and arrows are the agent by which Shiva shoots its powerful will and destroys imperfection and creates the new.

Sixth plane. The sixth plane is the realm of hyperconsciousness and the gamma ray frequency band. In this plane the awareness of being one with the whole of life is experienced.

Sixth seal. This seal is associated with the pineal gland and the gamma ray frequency band. The reticular formation that filters and veils the knowingness of the subconscious mind is opened when this seal is activated. The opening of the brain refers to the opening of this seal and the activation of its consciousness and energy.

Social consciousness. It is the consciousness of the second plane and the infrared frequency band. It is also called the image of the human personality and the mind of the first three seals. Social consciousness refers to the collective consciousness of human society. It is the collection of thoughts, assumptions, judgments, prejudices, laws, morality, values, attitudes, ideals, and emotions of the fraternity of the human race.

Soul. Ramtha refers to the soul as the Book of Life, where the whole journey of involution and evolution of the individual is recorded in the form of wisdom.

Subconscious mind. The seat of the subconscious mind is the lower cerebellum or reptilian brain. This part of the brain has its own independent connections to the frontal lobe and the whole of the body and has the power to access the mind of God, the wisdom of the ages.

Superconsciousness. This is the consciousness of the fifth plane and the x-ray frequency band.

Tahumo. Tahumo is the discipline taught by Ramtha in which the student learns the ability to master the effects of the natural environment — cold and heat — on the human body.

Tank field. It is the name of the large field with the labyrinth that is used for the discipline of The Tank^SM.

Tank^SM, The. It is the name given to the labyrinth used as part of the disciplines of Ramtha's School of Enlightenment. The students are taught to find the entry to this labyrinth blindfolded and move through it focusing on the Void without touching the walls or using the eyes or the senses. The objective of this discipline is to find, blindfolded, the center of the labyrinth or a room designated and representative of the Void.

Third plane. This is the plane of conscious awareness and the visible light frequency band. It is also known as the light plane and the mental plane. When the energy of the Blue Plane is lowered down to this frequency band, it splits into positive and negative polarity. It is at this point that the soul splits into two, giving origin to the phenomenon of soulmates.

Third seal. This seal is the energy center of conscious awareness and the visible light frequency band. It is associated with control, tyranny, victimization, and power. It is located in the region of the solar plexus.

Thought. Thought is different from consciousness. The brain processes a stream of consciousness modifying it into segments — holographic pictures — of neurological, electrical, and chemical prints called thoughts. Thoughts are the building blocks of mind.

Twilight™ ^SM. This term is used to describe the discipline taught by Ramtha in which the students learn to put their bodies in a catatonic state similar to deep sleep, yet retaining their conscious awareness.

Twilight™ ^SM Visualization Process. It is the process used to practice the discipline of the List or other visualization formats.

Ultraconsciousness. It is the consciousness of the seventh plane and the Infinite Unknown frequency band. It is the consciousness of an ascended master.

Unknown God. The Unknown God was the single God of Ramtha's ancestors, the Lemurians. The Unknown God also represents the forgotten divinity and divine origin of the human person.

Upper four seals. The upper four seals are the fourth, fifth, sixth, and seventh seals.

Void, the. The Void is defined as one vast nothing materially, yet all things potentially.

Yellow brain. The yellow brain is Ramtha's name for the neocortex, the house of analytical and emotional thought. The reason why it is called the yellow brain is because the neocortices were colored yellow in the original two-dimensional, caricature-style drawing Ramtha used for his teaching on the function of the brain and its processes. He explained that the different aspects of the brain in this particular drawing are exaggerated and colorfully highlighted for the sake of study and understanding. This specific drawing became the standard tool used in all the subsequent teachings on the brain.

Yeshua ben Joseph. Ramtha refers to Jesus Christ by the name Yeshua ben Joseph, following the Jewish traditions of that time.

FIG. A: THE SEVEN SEALS:
SEVEN LEVELS OF CONSCIOUSNESS IN THE HUMAN BODY

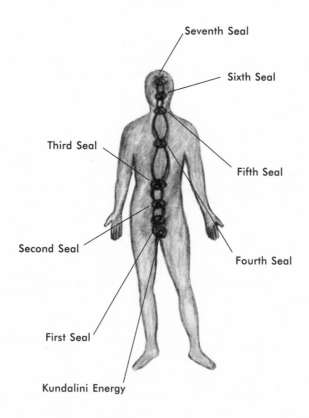

Seventh Seal

Sixth Seal

Third Seal

Fifth Seal

Second Seal

Fourth Seal

First Seal

Kundalini Energy

FIG. B: SEVEN LEVELS OF CONSCIOUSNESS AND ENERGY

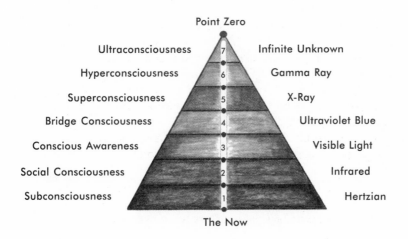

Point Zero

Ultraconsciousness	7	Infinite Unknown
Hyperconsciousness	6	Gamma Ray
Superconsciousness	5	X-Ray
Bridge Consciousness	4	Ultraviolet Blue
Conscious Awareness	3	Visible Light
Social Consciousness	2	Infrared
Subconsciousness	1	Hertzian

The Now

FIG. C: THE BRAIN

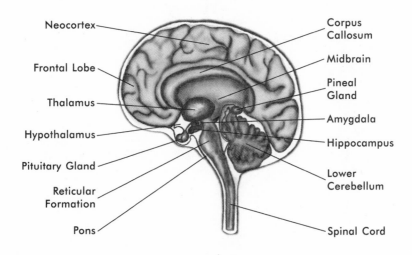

Neocortex
Frontal Lobe
Thalamus
Hypothalamus
Pituitary Gland
Reticular Formation
Pons

Corpus Callosum
Midbrain
Pineal Gland
Amygdala
Hippocampus
Lower Cerebellum
Spinal Cord

FIG. D: BINARY MIND — LIVING THE IMAGE

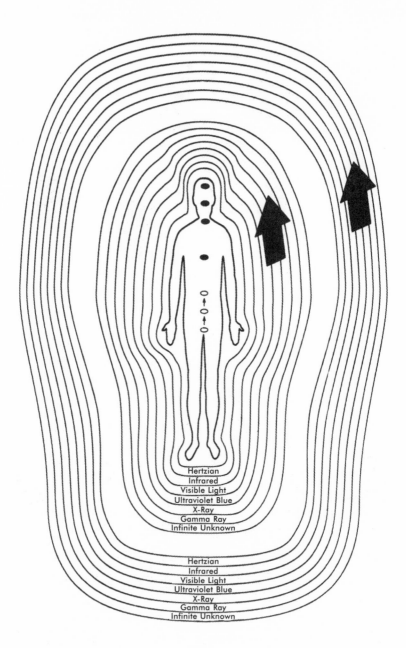

Hertzian
Infrared
Visible Light
Ultraviolet Blue
X-Ray
Gamma Ray
Infinite Unknown

Hertzian
Infrared
Visible Light
Ultraviolet Blue
X-Ray
Gamma Ray
Infinite Unknown

FIG. E: ANALOGICAL MIND — LIVING IN THE NOW

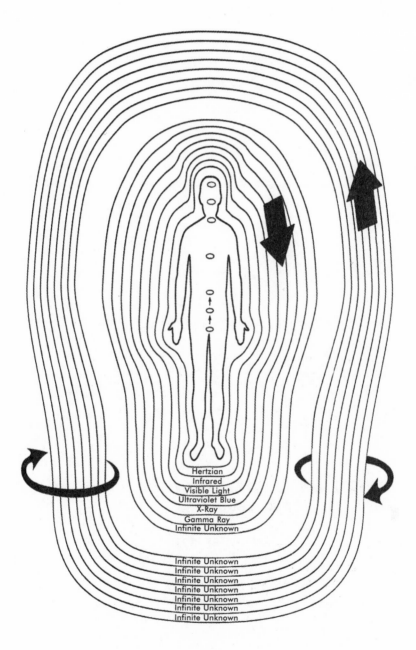

Hertzian
Infrared
Visible Light
Ultraviolet Blue
X-Ray
Gamma Ray
Infinite Unknown

Infinite Unknown
Infinite Unknown
Infinite Unknown
Infinite Unknown
Infinite Unknown
Infinite Unknown
Infinite Unknown

Ramtha's School of Enlightenment,
THE SCHOOL OF ANCIENT WISDOM

A Division of JZK, Inc.
P.O. Box 1210
Yelm, Washington 98597
360.458.5201
800.347.0439
www.ramtha.com
www.jzkpublishing.com